$11.00

LEARNING ABOUT THE EARTH
Tide Pools

by Colleen Sexton

BELLWETHER MEDIA • MINNEAPOLIS, MN

Note to Librarians, Teachers, and Parents:

Blastoff! Readers are carefully developed by literacy experts and combine standards-based content with developmentally appropriate text.

Level 1 provides the most support through repetition of high-frequency words, light text, predictable sentence patterns, and strong visual support.

Level 2 offers early readers a bit more challenge through varied simple sentences, increased text load, and less repetition of high-frequency words.

Level 3 advances early-fluent readers toward fluency through increased text and concept load, less reliance on visuals, longer sentences, and more literary language.

Level 4 builds reading stamina by providing more text per page, increased use of punctuation, greater variation in sentence patterns, and increasingly challenging vocabulary.

Level 5 encourages children to move from "learning to read" to "reading to learn" by providing even more text, varied writing styles, and less familiar topics.

Whichever book is right for your reader, Blastoff! Readers are the perfect books to build confidence and encourage a love of reading that will last a lifetime!

This edition first published in 2009 by Bellwether Media.

No part of this publication may be reproduced in whole or in part without written permission of the publisher. For information regarding permission, write to Bellwether Media Inc., Attention: Permissions Department, Post Office Box 19349, Minneapolis, MN 55419.

Library of Congress Cataloging-in-Publication Data
Sexton, Colleen A., 1967–
   Tide pools / by Colleen Sexton.
      p. cm. – (Blastoff! readers. Learning about the earth)
   Includes bibliographical references and index.
   Summary: "Simple text and full color photographs introduce beginning readers to the characteristics and geographical locations of tide pools. Developed by literacy experts for students in kindergarten through third grade"–Provided by publisher.
   ISBN-13: 978-1-60014-231-4 (hardcover : alk. paper)
   ISBN-10: 1-60014-231-1 (hardcover : alk. paper)
   1. Tide pool ecology–Juvenile literature. 2. Tide pools–Juvenile literature. I. Title.

QH541.5.S35S47 2009
577.69'9–dc22   2008013326

Contents

Tide pools form on rocky shores by the ocean.

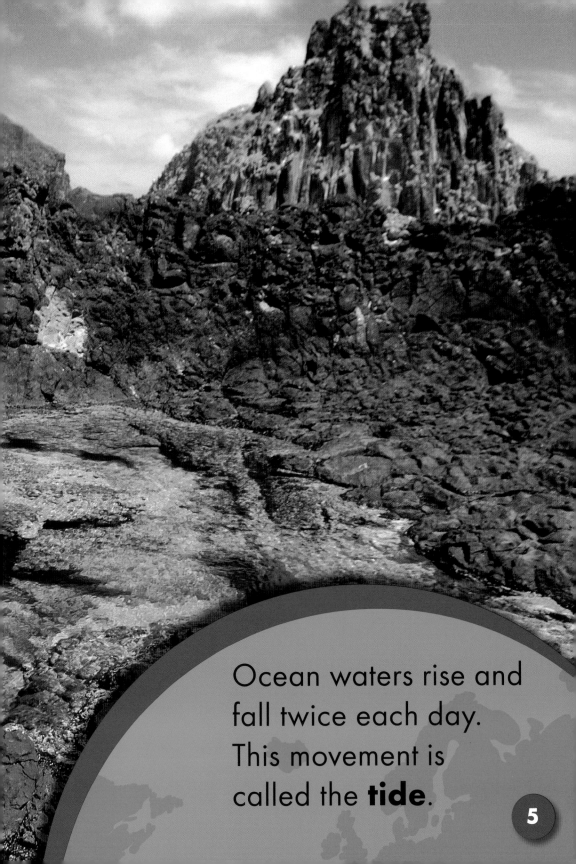

Ocean waters rise and fall twice each day. This movement is called the **tide**.

5

Water rushes onto shore during high tide. Water covers much of the shore.

Water moves away from shore during low tide. The shore becomes part of the land again.

Sometimes water stays on the shore at low tide. It fills **hollows** in the rocks. These hollows become tide pools.

Tide pools that are high on the shore are usually small and **shallow**. Tide pools that are closer to the water can be large and deep.

Tide pools are full of life. Some plants and animals wash in and out with the tide. Others live there all the time.

Tide pools can be dangerous places to live. A strong wave can carry away or crush plants and animals. However, some have found ways to stay safe in a tide pool.

Kelp, Irish moss, and other **seaweed** stick to rocks with a **holdfast**. A holdfast keeps the seaweed from washing away.

Some animals grab hold of rocks. Sea stars use suckers on their tube feet to hold on to rocks. Snails hang on with their one big foot.

Other animals stay safe from waves in other ways. Shrimp and small fish hide in cracks in the rocks. Sea urchins squeeze their prickly bodies between rocks.

Mussels make thick, sticky threads that attach them to rocks. Crabs crawl under thick, wet seaweed.

During low tide, the sun's heat can dry up tide pools. Animals must find ways to stay wet.

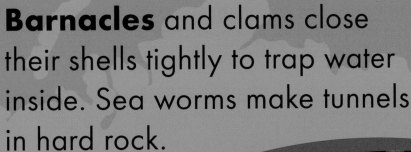

Barnacles and clams close their shells tightly to trap water inside. Sea worms make tunnels in hard rock.

Sea anemones pull in their wet **tentacles** to keep them from drying in the air.

Many tide pool animals breathe **oxygen** in the water. They need oxygen to live. During low tide, animals can use up nearly all of the oxygen in the water.

High tide brings fresh oxygen to the tide pool. It also brings food. Millions of tiny, clear creatures called **plankton** drift in on the tide.

The plankton are a feast
for many of the hungry
tide pool animals!

Glossary

barnacle—an ocean animal with a hard shell that attaches itself to clams, rocks, ships, and even whales; a barnacle stays where it is attached for its whole life.

holdfast—a rootlike body part that holds some types of seaweed to rocks and other hard surfaces

hollow—an empty space; a place where the ground is lower than other land around it.

oxygen—a gas that animals need to survive

plankton—tiny creatures that float in the ocean and are food for other animals; plankton are too small to be seen with the naked eye.

seaweed—a type of algae that grows in the ocean

shallow—not deep

tentacles—the long, thin arms of some sea animals

tide—the regular rise and fall of ocean waters; water rises at high tide and lowers at low tide.

To Learn More

AT THE LIBRARY

Brenner, Barbara. *One Small Place by the Sea*. New York: HarperCollins, 2004.

Halpern, Monica. *All About Tide Pools*. Washington, D.C.: National Geographic, 2007.

Hodgkins, Fran. *Between the Tides*. Camden, Maine: Down East Books, 2007.

ON THE WEB

Learning more about tide pools is as easy as 1, 2, 3.

1. Go to www.factsurfer.com

2. Enter "tide pools" into search box.

3. Click the "Surf" button and you will see a list of related web sites.

With factsurfer.com, finding more information is just a click away.

Index

The images in this book are reproduced through the courtesy of: Chris Cheadle / age fotostock, front cover, pp. 8-9; Andre Seale / age fotostock, pp. 4-5; rollie rodriguez / Alamy, p. 6; Michael Howell / Alamy, p. 7; George Grall / Getty Images, pp. 10, 14-15, 20-21; Visual&Written SL / Alamy, pp. 12, 13; Mark Conlin / V&W / imagequestmarine.com, p. 16; Carly Rose Hennigan, p. 17; Georgette Douwma / Getty Images, p. 18.